Find Me in the Forest

Poems and Ponderings of
Nature, Consciousness, and Self

By Ashley Lynn

Copyright

Copyright 2022 © Ashley Lynn
Adventures Across LLC

No part of this issue may be copied, distributed, or reposted without prior permission from the author and publisher.

All poems & ponderings here were created by the author, Ashley Lynn, and are meant to be blips of truths to help you reach your own divine truth.

Illustrations, cover, and book format by Ashley Lynn

ISBN: 978-1-7342121-5-0

Dedication

To all humans on Earth right now,

To all the commoners that run the show,

To all the star souls who showed up here,

To all way showers who lead the way for humanity,

To all the light workers sharing the light,

Thank you for being here and sharing your love.

This poetry book is for you.

Make your life the best one yet.

I love you.

Acknowledgements

There are many people I'd like to thank for their support in my journey as a self-published author, artist, & Earth experiencer.

Many of these poems & ponderings were written on my excursions to other places. These excursions wouldn't have been possible without the hospitality and opportunities from open & lovely folks. Thank you **Sue, Michelle, Thomas, Lou Ann, Jenny & Bob** for giving me a safe place to rest, inspiring places to create, and opportunities to live and grow.

I'd like to extend thanks to my **mom, siblings,** and **grandparents** for loving me unconditionally throughout this process of becoming who I am, and for always allowing me to follow my path even if it is different. I so appreciate your gentleness and care in being supportive and encouraging with me!

To my **father** who has now passed, thank you for being supportive of me until the end of your physical life here, and thank you for being with me in the ethers as I continue my life here. Our soul connection is strong and I know you always have my back, no matter what happens. Thank you for guiding me as a child on the path of integrity, honesty, passion, and humbleness as these are such valuable qualities I can practice in my life now. Though I cannot see you anymore, I feel your love, support, and pride in me as I continue to follow my path.

A special thanks to **Morgan S.** for your encouragement and continuous support on my self-published author journey. You've been my #1 fan and friend since the very beginning from my first book and I am so grateful for your genuine & motherly heart alongside mine. Extending that thanks to **Sierra, Cat, Mark, Steph, Kimmy, Ange, Tina, Eric, and to all I've met on the internet** who I've shared conversation with about Adventures Across. Your feedback, friendliness, and support keep me going as a creator!

Thank you to my dear friends in my community who have made me feel at home here. Thank you **Paul, Paula, Kathleen, Eileen, Kacey, Cree, Cassondra, Jenny, and Kathy** for spending time with me and giving my cosmic soul space to expand and be here, and allowing me safety in the comfort of your homes.

Thank you **Austin** for being with me everyday by my side, and for helping me with practical things like proofreading, marketing, cooking, cleaning, and adventuring. I couldn't have asked for a better life-partner than you, and being able to have fun everyday inspires my work and to keep on my path. It is a true blessing to have written many of these poems and ponderings with you by my side somewhere, combing some riverbed for stones or hiking up mountains in the desert. I'm so grateful for the adventurous and child-spirit you are.

A heartfelt thanks to my team of friends and acquaintances who helped me edit and launch this book to the world. I couldn't have done this without you, and your time and support have been so meaningful to me as a self-published author.

Thank you **Mother Earth** for giving me such a beautiful and bountiful place to live, evolve, and create. You inspired many of these poems with your wisdom and colors, and I'm grateful to be a caretaker for you while I'm here.

And thank YOU dear soul who agreed to come to Earth at this time, voluntarily or not, to raise the vibration and consciousness of this planet. Your service here is greatly appreciated and is rippling out into the cosmos. Your presence here is making a much bigger impact than you can see with your two eyes - remember that! We couldn't do this without you! I honor you and your path. Let yourself be free here.

Other Books by Ashley Lynn

A Year Against the Rain
Lessons Learned Living Off-Grid on the Oregon Coast

Morning Motivations
Uplifting Poetry & Photography to Start Your Day

The Adventures Across Guided Journal

The Adventures Across Zine
Op. 1 - Earth Encyclopedia
Op. 2 - Sacred Symbology

And more to come...

Table of Contents

Nature 3

    The Purpose of Winter 4
    Blizzard Beauty 5
    Golden Winter 7
    Energies of Februaries 8
    Woodpecker Wisdom 12
    The Late Winter Squall 13
    Oracle Orchards 18
    Seasoning Transitioning 19
    Spirits of the Stars 20
    Senses in Surroundings 21
    A Morning in May 22
    Forest of Flowers 23
    I Often Think 26
    Winds of Change 27
    Into the Woods 27
    Hoverfly 28
    Ocean Breeze 29
    Grand Canyon 30
    Raven Message 30
    Mother Nature is an Artist 31
    Fear of Cities 32
    Forest Spirits 36
    River Release 37
    A Dream is a Seed 38
    The Day 39
    Sensuality 40
    The Smell of Oxygen 42
    Cow Bird Call 44
    Late Summer Prairie 45
    Fall is Coming 46
    The Secret World of Frogs 47
    Bridge Birch Reflection 48

Consciousness 51

    Nostalgia Time Travel 52
    Two Friends 54
    Awareness 55
    Signs 60
    Naked Showers 62
    Exploring 64

Creation Station 65
The Rise of the Feminine 66
Energies of Earth 68
Charging Crystals for Drinks 68
Friends Forever 69
Ponderings 70
Ask ❋ Believe ❋ Prepare ❋ Receive 71
How to Manifest 72
Mirror Effect 74
Stillness 75
You Led Me Here 78
Point 78
Earth Encyclopedia 79
Talking to the Universe 80
Insects Into the Lights 81
Abundance Flow 82
What if…? 83
Full Moon Cleanse 84
Intergalactic Hug 85
Tranquility 86
A Day with the Heart 87
Song of Your Soul 88
Inner Divinity 88
When one door closes, another one opens. 89
Things of Thoughts 90
Remember 90
Desires & Regrets 90
Why so Sirius? 91
Days of Old 92
Sovereignty 93
Mirrors Remember 94
Quartz Crystals 95
Something Grounding 96
Treasure Chest 97
Skin & Bones 97
Gardening Scene 98
A Message of Gratitude 100

Self 103

Doubts 105
Mirage Tune - A Song 107
Memories Song 108
Live large 110
Inner Song 111

Flow and Flux	111
Seeds	112
Wonder	112
Personal Vow	113
You're the Sun	113
Forgiveness of the Moment	114
Faulty Failures	116
Love is	118
A Midnight Pondering	119
Open Eyes, Open Heart	120
Celebration Contemplation	121
Mirrors	124
Comparing and Sharing	124
Sundays	125
Free Spirit	126
When the Going Gets Rough	127
Truth Chant	129
Beginning the Truth	129
Resilience	130
Are You Ready?	131
The Heart of Winter	132
Uncertainty and Faith	133
Surrender	133
Be Deciduous	133
Warrior	134
Feel Into Yourself	135
Personal Truth	136
Your Time	137
Be Like a River	138
You're Enough	140
Content	141
Shadow Self	142
Shadow	142
Rest	143
Strange Me	144
Sweet Surrender	145
Moving On	146
Emotions	147
A Lasting Reminder	148
Visit Adventures Across Online!	151

Introduction

Inside this little book are a collection of poems & ponderings I've been writing since 2017.

I wrote these poems & ponderings during a five year exploratory time in my life while nomading around America. After college, my partner and I experimented and sought out to learn about alternative ways of living, spirituality, and consciousness. We had a dream to be sovereign and free in our own unique way and lived off grid, worked on an organic farm, stayed in a sacred site for a few years, traveled, and decided to bring all the knowledge home to Wisconsin to build our own slice of heaven on planet Earth.

Writing poetry has been a cathartic way for me to ground my experiences in nature and my self, what I feel, wisdom I've picked up, and to express creativity. It is something my soul enjoys, making sense of this reality we live in.

These poems & ponderings are of a range of topics, from the magic in nature, to the knowledge from the cosmos, light hearted ways of living, the infinite world of consciousness, meeting with ethereal beings, motivations to pursue your dreams, and contemplations for integrating emotions. Some poems are long and introspective, others work as a sort of mantra you can bring along with you during your days. I've organized the poems & ponderings in sections **NATURE - CONSCIOUSNESS - & SELF** so that you can easily flip to if you're looking for a string of thought pertaining to something.

I am happiest and most myself when I'm in the forest and nature. Often times it is hard for me to speak what goes on internally, so I meander off into the forest and talk to the trees, flowers, and faeries. Being a sensitive and spiritual soul, I can tune into energies and chat with ethereal beings, sometimes better than humans. Since I wrote most of this poetry out in wild places, I've named the book "Find Me in the Forest," because, well, if you can't find me, that's probably where I am. My soul's home.

In addition to writing poetry and books, I'm an avid nature photographer, having more photos of flowers than a person truly needs... Many of the illustrations within this book are line drawings of my photographs from my travels. Others are just doodles to accompany the poetry.

May these poems serve you well on your journey here on Earth. Imagine the whimsy of nature with me, in each picture painted with words. Pull out this book when you need inspiration, something to relate to, or a companion.

Much love to you on your journey,

Ashley Lynn

Nature

The Purpose of Winter

In winter, the sky glows ethereal pastels

Soft periwinkles & lavenders, like feathery petals

These colors bring us to a dreamy place

Seen between the skeletons of trees

A place where everything & nothing exists

A place the soul exists & persists

That eventually comes back to Earth

In a form that gives you bliss

Blizzard Beauty

In the silence of the wood,
A subtle voice is loudly heard
The pithing of crystals crashing against trees
Makes me aware of other worlds around me

How peculiar that snow hitting bark
Can create such a noise, a sure spark
Sound is a thing invisible but there
Consciousness without form & presence like a bear

As infinite individuals fall to the ground
Piling up, silence their only sound
I'm reminded of impact of numbers
Each light-being creating ripples in the waters

Each being living soul led lives
Creates a new Earth, a new paradigm

While we envision
And make heart-felt decisions
We'll wake up one day and realize
The beauty of a blizzard before our eyes

Sunshine Storage

Isn't it comforting feeling the warm sun in the dead of winter?

Oh the trees
That store the heat
Deep
In their wood a'splintered

I thank them, for gathering the heat
To keep me warm, my feet
In the cold & early morn

A beautiful blessin',
A lesson
Of many cycles occurring at a second

Winter is like a death, an end of a season
Of planting, growing, harvesting within reason

As the wood burns, so does a spark
Of a new chance to follow my heart

Every dead thing is useful to somebody
Deceased leaves really throw a mycelium party

Just as the cured wood heats up my soul
A new dream is born, soon to be a'glow

Golden Winter

Golden Winter
You're Summer's sister
Her laughter
Like a silent whisper

Energies of Februaries

February is like being at the bottom of an ocean
Dark, still, stagnant, but a slight breeze of an undertow
And normally this time of year I would be at whits end
But this undertow makes me feel like life is in hidden flow

When what I do in a day is relax, contemplate, and stay home,
I'm in inner mode,
feeling things that happened a long time ago

A brighter light shines upon them,
the undertow,
they're no longer traumas but things that form
who I am today, my normal norm

Everything makes sense now,
February the month of hidden scenes under my skin
Contemplating my life yet again

February, my favorite and least favorite month of the year
You're an ocean I swim through
to sift through
the old me to create my authentic truth

This year feels lighter,
My path a little clearer

A sensation of walking through life with a weightless back
when in the past, it was heavier than seven lifetimes of crap

As I simmer in this moment for what seems like forever
I continue on my way, down my path today, light as a feather,
spirit cleansed with the weather

And ascend to the light at the end of February

Sunshine in February

Once again
The sun
She peers above the ridge

Chickadees change their tune
    announcing spring is arriving soon
The warmth of her rays
    bring my heart joy
    for flowery days
Suddenly I feel hopeful again
    after months in a dark shadow
    the mountain cast over our home
Dreams of trilliums enter my mind
    Dutchman's breeches, spring's first sign
    and fairy potatoes
    between thick tree roots
    fresh shades of green
    of young fern shoots

Tree trunks roll down
    the hill, decades of sound
Grumbles into the ground
    for the mycelium, they have found

The sun, she moves across the sky
    as for February, I will try
To cherish each day, a moment in time
    with the new found light
    in my window it shines

Feet in a Cold Creek

'Twas a springy day in February
Delightful, unusual on the contrary
    when we headed into town

Sunlight reflected off the snow
Casting warmth to our faces a'glow
    drip drops fall from rooftops to the ground

Social dog parents, to whom we chatter
Sharing quirkiness and laughter
    lighthearted encounters, a saunter

Soon after, in our horseless carriage we leave
Down a hard, hilly path in the trees
    therein opens a valley with a stream

Out the door springs Sparky
Personality, a bit barky
    to the kinkling water below

"Let's cross!" I grinned
On the other bank, was brimmed
    with crystals amongst river stones

"Here's a path we can take,"
Austin's toes tipped, he'd make
    it across quite effortlessly

I was quick to follow behind
Surely, I wasn't blind
    the path to the other side easy

Immediately I did find
Glittery stones made by time
    and fusing together sand & mineral

Oh my how they sparkle!
Druzy quartz a faery wonder
    full of elemental power

Despite the freezing temperature
I cast my bare feet in magic water
    my body coming alive

Austin returned to me, so slick
"I brought you a wishing stick!
      make a wish and cast it astride."

I closed my eyes, shut tight
I imagined a bright ethereal light
      around my heart desire so true

Together we cast our dried goldenrod
Into the rushing creek with a nod
      away our dreams went into the blue

Alas, it was time to go
I put my boots on in the snow
      and wrote this memory here for you

Woodpecker Wisdom

Have you ever noticed that when a hairy woodpecker dines at your bird feeder, she is actually using her tongue to drive it into the ball pen of seeds inside to pull one out, to only obliterate the seed and to go in for more?

Woodpeckers are quite the opportunists. Downy & Hairy have similar temperaments, being more selfish it seems in nature & pecking at the chickadees and finches who wish for a taste of food too. Yet, Jimmy, our red-bellied friend glows crimson at his base, sharing there's enough for all and shares more willingly with his bird companions.

These fluffy friends are brave, resilient, assertive, and opportunists, sticking around for the harsh winters & thriving in the forest as they do. Have you noticed that they will peck at trees for hours, creating holes inside that make homes for other birds and animals? Just for a bite to eat! Opportunists to say the least... The next time you see a woodpecker, give them a nod. And know that you have these qualities within you too.

The Late Winter Squall

I was informed we were having a squall
I chuckled a little, silly faery me
Had no idea what a squall was after all

My pen traced the trees
Then all of a sudden, a gusty breeze!
Nearly knocked me to the ground
Laughing, so funny, at my knees

Weather extremes
Always entertain me so
And I was to find out what a squall was
Rushing to the back door to go

Gusty winds, piercingly fast like a storm at sea
The birds quickly eat then hide
While the chimes tweedle-dee

All at once, hail, rain, sleet, & snow
I, laying on the back porch watched the trees to & fro

For a moment, a breezy silence
Then "WHOOSH" oaks creaked in the distance
My spirit came alive
Feeling the soul of the pine,
Outside
My window

Cracked hands shuffled the chopped wood in
A grimace from my face
Winds of change, allow me to create again

A funny thing, how creativity flows
Squalls come in to bring magic to my soul

The forest, she danced with me
Our stiff joints moved, and we were set free

Geese Fly into Sound

A lost friend came into view, it's been eight years since I've seen you

Hiking on these old trails, lifts the veils,
    of time lost

Good times, create good vibes,
    of a friendship everlasting

The day was ending, but we were sending,
    our souls into the sounds

The sounds of color, we were to discover,
    weren't imaginary after all

We shared how home was best,
    no matter where in the world we'd the chance to rest

Traveling is fun, as long as you don't run,
    from the thing your soul needs most

We are geese, nomads at the least,
    looking for our soul and purpose

Upon a bridge, on the lake's ridge,
    we discovered the sounds of color

The sounds of color, we are to discover,
    are the potions to healing the past

Staring at the sunset, capturing the wonderment,
    with a mirror and a lens

Watch the geese go by, and you really try,
    to capture them in frame

Moments go by, but we can try,
    to hang onto them with a photo

Let's create art, it's a start,
    to a life of everlasting

No matter where you are, near or far,
    you will always be in my heart

Let you discover, the sounds of color,
    in the Midwest sunset scene

Tulip

Oh tulip, early to bloom
Your sweet scent made me fall for you

Your petals are the feathers
of a cardinal so red
Drooping over top of me
to wistfully kiss my head

Your song is so cheery
brightening anyone's day
Bees come a'buzzing
to keep sadness at bay

The last of your nectar
so sweet and so kind
It fills with joy in the
heart, soul, and mind

Oh tulip, how I love you so
For you teach me lessons
Of life as we both grow

Trees Have Eyes

Have you ever noticed how trees have eyes?
They are always watching, so very alive
Wide open, many so wise
Even at night, to receive the fireflies

What if one day, their eye blinks?
Their roots come up and the soil below sinks?
Trees walking down the streets
Branches lift up to wave with leaves

What a sight that would be
Or,
Don't we experience this already?

Oracle Orchards

I found a grove of fruit trees
Interspersed in the forest deep
Plums, apples, and cherries
Resting here on their own, merry

Or did somebody plant them long ago?
Planting orchards near forests to grow
Placed by settlers from afar who moved here
Engulfed by wild foliage, later a hundred years

Yes this is the essence of a food forest
Created naturally or by a folklorist
A forest that had all the essentials for eating
And simple pleasures for a life completing

Beyond the crooked trees
you will see vast biodiversity
Hundreds of types of bees and wasps
That in a corn field appear to be lost

As I sit among the whispering trees
I realize
Humans don't need to do anything to be happy
To be fed
To be healthy
They just need to sit, watch, and be

Seasoning Transitioning

I was afraid to leave early spring behind
The days filled with slow blooming
A looming
That summer was on its way.

The gentle reminder that winter still hung on
While spring just woke up from the late evening sun

Until today, a warm fragrant day
The plum trees filled with pungent white flowers
And the sweet apple blossoms
Oh how they make my heart feel lovely!

And the light touch of a minute spider
traversing through my arm hairs

Everything is sprouting so quickly
I just want to push pause on the moment
And really capture in my memories
Of this stunning May day

Spirits of the Stars

Are flowers

just the

Earthly spirits of the stars?

Senses in Surroundings

Have you ever felt velvety spring leaves
from a maple tree?
Or stumbled upon a land with such fresh fragrance
it made you want to dance?

Columbines droop with their melancholy of spring leaving us
The seasons not separate but a flow that we must trust

Flitters grace down a towering apple tree
Petals blanketing the ground
Reminiscent of a bride's gown
I can't help but to sit in the essence

Choke cherries stick their floral fingers out
A reminder to stop and smell the flowers

Beautiful days like today
Remind me to sit in simple presence

A Morning in May

A crimson dew drop lifts over the horizon
Everywhere, blotches of color go a'flyin
A symphony of sounds echo the valley
The summer birds are back, impossible to tally

Nature's bakery, a smell-ery, is open
Scents are all free! No need for a token
The pillowy scent of wild plum so sweet
A comfort transmuted to coolness for the afternoon heat

Apply blossoms, growing in groups of five
Share stories with me of their land in another time
How things change yet still remain the same
Is that paradox that can take away pain

The understory boasts greens of all the glory
Little leaves about to tell their story
Of all the time that's passed, all the things they've seen
Are all stored in their colors so green

We can know anything, all we have to do is ask
The whole process is such a simple task
Close your eyes, & focus your intent on
That which you seek, in a mind so calm
The answers flow in like a calming breeze
In your mind's eye, where all can be seen

Imagination is our greatest superpower
A magician's task, one accessed at any hour
We all have this power, don't you see?
We are all creators of enchanted realities

Forest of Flowers

Pitter patter
Leaves they chatter
As I inch along the forest floor

Wind, it swept
Through the garden well kept
By the faeries forevermore

A forest of flowers
Enchanted by cosmic powers
Wakes at the coming of spring

Many expressions unique
Variations seen in their physique
Colors, how loudly they sing

Trilliums with their petals of three
Radiate true balance and purity

Then there's Jack in the Pulpit
Whose goblet is the gossip culprit

Apple blossoms perfume the air
The angelic five reaching out with care

Hepatica with their violet petals of six
Show us the first signs of spring bliss

Spring beauties are such tiny cuties
Pink velvets of innocence, rarely moody

Behold! The grand essence of March marigold!
Clusters so thick, a vibrance of pure gold

Flowers are so infinite & plenty
Encounters with them are full and ready

Each with an essence,
Of pure consciousness
A friend for me, that is a fact

Earthing

Touch your bare feet to the ground
Feel who it is that is around

Silence your mind and intently listen
To the voices that carry throughout the wind

What is it that they say to you?
Friendly advice that'll enable you to move through...

Feel the trees' roots a distance away
And dance with our quiet friends as they sway

A miracle moment you will discover
The trees are alive and very empowered

Move your feet across the damp land
Then make your way to the river bed's sand

Pick up a rock and state the feelings
You want to let go of, the no-serving things

Throw the rock into the stream
Those parts of you are gone, it's time to dream!

Set your intentions and cast them into the wind
Remember this day on the day you win

Take some time today to unplug from the hustle before you
Your soul needs this to align to the truest version of you

Rudbeckia

Sometimes we cannot see our impact
As our vibrations cannot be seen

As Rudbeckia grows tall & sways in the wind
Her flowers open and gaze toward the sun
She may never see the impact on those below
Though
She has not eyes, but a soul

The observer can see
A wolf spider's nest, but three
With hundreds of babies, so tiny
Housed between Rudbeckia's leaves

Or what about the lines of ants?
Crawling up her hairy stem
Creating farms of aphids underneath
To return later, for a tasty treat

Still Rudbeckia strives to be with the sun
Her petals out wide, golden fun
Her vibrations for life radiate about her
Creating ripples out into the ethers

Become an observer in your life
To see the bigger picture of your impact
Just because nobody can see you
Does not mean your life is blue

You are like Rudbeckia, have not only eyes that see
Remember the soul, and the large flower you are to be

I Often Think

I often think
That if humans kept on destroying the planet
Who would be the one worse off
Humans, or Earth?
Humans need Earth to survive.
But Earth doesn't necessarily need humans

Take for example an abandoned mansion
The humans are all gone
But nature adapted, came in and now inhabits a ghost of a house

In my opinion, it is not Earth that is in danger
It is us
We are doomed by our own ways
Unless we can change

If we go back in history and look at how simply people lived
And how happy they were with what they had
You'd realize that you already have more than them.
Our technology can help us in many ways
But we can still be simple folk
We don't need things to make us happy
We need each other, healthy food, and love...
love for each other and ourselves
We need our passions, the things that make us excited to live
We need nature, we need Earth,
because we are in fact little pieces of Earth creatively crafted together

We don't need to keep building and developing
We don't need every franchise in every town
Why is it that humans recently crave monoculture in every category of life?
Isn't diversity more interesting and fun?

Ask yourself these questions the next time you decide to go to the supermarket for groceries rather than the local co-op who carries food from the local farmers in your area.

Just remember this
It is not Earth that needs saving
It is us.
Save US.

Winds of Change

When the winds of change blow
Go with the flow

Into the Woods

Into the woods we go
To uncover a part of our souls
Under the moss we find
A 'shroom!
I have his heart
And he has mine

Ocean's waves, she flows
Up on shore rushing fast,
though afar pushing slow

She shares with us that life can be both
Fast and slow, eb and flow
A chance to surrender and to let go

Hoverfly

I met a hover fly amongst a stand of desert asters
A magical experience, though for others flies can be a pester

I stand so still, like my friends the cacti
Hoping that this fly wouldn't pass me by

He came to inspect,
behind me he went
The buzzing rattling through my nerves

A giggle I let out,
like a little worm wiggle
And he flew away without a sound

I sat upon a rock and looked at my friends around me
The wind was so still but they moved ever so slightly!

As if to say, "Hello, I'm with you today human fellow!
I notice you and feel your energy too"

As I breathe out, you breathe in
We exchange with each other CO_2 and oxygen

Deep in connection with my plant friends
The hover fly, oh he was back again!

This time he decided to come up close
Looking straight into my left eye, a moment in time froze!

I let out a laugh, this guy was a hoot!
How much he trusted me he showed as he moved
The plants swayed in glee, as the sun shone through the trees
& our little gathering
ended
when I stood up to return home

Ocean Breeze

You know that feeling of salt sticking to the air on your hands?
And trekking on a path no one has been through, cracked
You enjoy the journey on the way
The simplest things give the most joy, I must say
Then you get to the top and see the whole ocean blue
It's a subtle reminder of how many possibilities are in from you

Grand Canyon

A river, rushing over bare land
Over time carved out of layers of hard sand

A canyon, jagged, a mile deep
Watch out that drop is steep!

Fast paced, though progress slow
It just kept on with its flow

Years and years later
Within the land is a carved out crater

Its message, impact subtly engrained
Humbling flowing, knowing its purpose was entertained

Raven Message

A raven, first time to me up close
As big as my dog, I suppose
Blinked his eyes and let out a crow
It appeared to me, he was speaking so

With each caw he let out,
Shoulders shrugged as he opened his mouth
Like saying "oh well, we have what we have,
Might as well be happy, instead of always sad."

With that, his easy message seeped into my skin
A kiss that helped me let go again

Mother Nature is an Artist

Mother Nature is an artist you know
So many brushes she has, I was told

Those perfect white whisps hanging in the air?
Why, she painted those with the tips of her hair!
By the way the wind steadily moves
You see the ends of bristles, in the cloud grooves

The sky isn't the only canvas
The earth itself has more to show us!
Not only is She a swift painter
Out of star dust, she creates wonders as a sculptor!
All of the forms of expression
Rise up out of the Earth without hesitation
Beings, so silent - in the breeze they sway
To four legged creatures, if you may...

But then there's the water
Whose form of art is that of an actor
Carrying, displaying vast emotions
Some will calm you, some cause commotion
Brilliant plays the water can put on
From action packed flowage, to catching the essence of dawn

Then she's the artist that started it all
The fire, passion, growing from being small
An idea, how brilliant!
Rising up out of the ashes, embodying resilience

And from something dead
Rises magnificence once again
Her creations allow us to live here
A planet so unique, I hold truly dear

Look around you, a free gallery to see
How blessed we all are, you and me

Mother Nature is an artist, you know
So many brushes she has, I was told.

Fear of Cities

Being a child of the wild
I often find myself scared of the cities
Not the actual city itself
But the spread of that city

The thought of concrete creeping up into the grasses
Brings a tear to my eye
Would that ever happen?
A city steamrolls, nature shrieks out and dies?

I want to buy land out in the country.
But how far away from a city, civilization, is safe to be?
Where the city wouldn't wash up in my front yard
And tell me it's time to move out
While I watch my beautiful farm get gobbled up
By grey, hard concrete and tall glass buildings...

What can we do
To keep the land safe?
Because I want to keep my land safe
Raw
Natural
Precisely imperfect as nature would have it
What do I have to do
To convince cities
To just stop building already?
We already have enough.
Enough is the planet

Flower Feels Reals

Being in a field of flowers feels so great because you have focused upon you hundreds of the same beings, the same essence, projecting their attention onto you, and showering you in complete bliss, unconditional love, and serenity.

Dandelion DNA

A dandelion is like an atom. There's the center point, the nucleus, the flower origination surrounded by a field of electrons, possibilities, represented as seeds. The seeds are possibilities as they are encoded with concentrated DNA to create a new dandelion, flower head, and it keeps going.

What seeds of possibilities are floating around you right now?

Intermission in Nature

Just sharing a little journey I had today
While in Wisconsin, the last day of my stay

The refreshing stench of a fishy pond
A smell I've come to be quite fond

The air, moist and warm like a fresh baked sponge cake
Hangs on my skin, wetness, to make me feel awake

Feathers litter the land of clovers, nettles, and yarrow
Enchanted land I can walk through, soaking up all my sorrow

The river is quick! Keeping the energy flowing
Reminding me that no matter how many emotions, I'll keep on growing

After strolling past a hedge
Of wild irises, forget me nots, and sedge

A bench called my name to come sit
To watch a pond and the ducks drift

Under the oaks, hickories, and birches I ponder
How beautiful life is, the magic, the wonder

A few words I murmur to a transformed friend
A promise that we will get to meet again

At that instant, a strange bird call
In bird talk, it could be a southern drawl

I turned around and what do I see?
A bright orange oriole, perched on an oak tree!

A rare bird for me to see,
I knew immediately,
It's message, a clear one to me.

With a heart filled with sincere gratitude
Pure abundance will have found its way to you.
The bird flew, and I followed behind
Something I've learned is to follow the signs

As I walked through slowly
I swear I heard a symphony

So many birds with different voices,
All perfect with their chirping noises

A tree with half its leaves,
I decided to bless with a moment of peace

This land was frozen to a crisp
During this last winter, one so brisk

Hidden bridges are new paths to walk upon
Oh how hidden opportunities come out of the mud...

As I finished my morning wandering
I realized what peace I get from aimless sauntering

This land I'll soon leave behind
But in my heart it remains a memory entwined

The smell of a flourishing pond

The millions of shades of green

The cheerful bird calls of the north

The taste of rich soil

And the touch of forget-me-nots on my heart

Forest Spirits

Whispers of the ethers bubble up
From layers and layers beneath the muck

Essences of purity trickle to the surface
Healing waters for all beings to nourish

Such whispers are otherworldly
To get here they've taken quite the journey

Listen to the whispers of the forest spirits, they know
The answers to all your questions, just ask them so

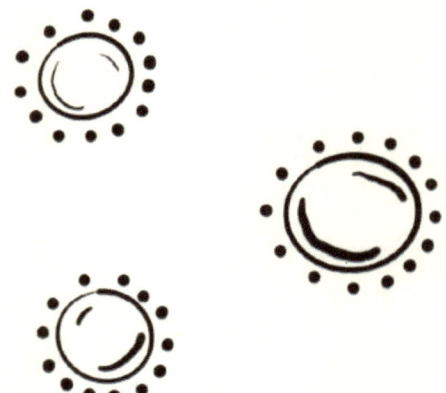

River Release

The lake looked as blue as the ocean, aquamarine to the touch

The river smelled this warming vibe and decided to join the lake in a swirly blue love

Purple hues swiftly drifted through the trees, glided across the rocky shore and ended with a trickle into the lake, like it was hesitant to give away its love to something so big and mysterious

The trees signaled that it was okay, their solace cast onto the surface of the gentle stream

Let go of fear and join this big body to become one

Embrace the unknown because that is all that is ever known

A Dream is a Seed

No matter how big or small,
a dream is a seed,
and that's not all

A seed that will bloom through
all the gloom
and grow into a tree so tall

The Day

I look forward to the day

When Mother Nature wraps her green vines upon every building

When man lets go of striving to be better

When existing in love is enough

When we look at one another and accept what we see
everyone is human, we are all the same
with our own unique beauty

When we look at the stars
and know in our hearts
that there's home among the constellations
the star systems

When we realize that we are here
to heal and to learn

When man and nature coexist,
aiding in the growth of one another

When meeting friends from far away,
is exciting and enlightening

When we communicate not with words,
but with our hearts

I look forward to the day

Sensuality

The rain sounds like the pearls of ocean sweat
As their precious beauty leave your scruffy face and absorb into my spongy skin

I spend all my days with you, smelling that green abundant air
being in nature's sexual energy
engulfed in her invisible arms of existence

But I feel most alive
most at home when I can see
the stars in your eyes
yours looking into mine

As we explore each other's vessels
without shame
but with unconditional acceptance

And I feel the layers peel off of me
my brokenness becomes whole
and I no longer feel so bad

What I see and love all day in the forest
is within you

The velvety flowers

The cry of the jay

The echoes of reaching grasses

The innocence of the understory

Transfer into me until I glow
and let it all go

Prairie Bed Love

An embrace with you, flowers
Igniting inside, powers
Of purity and passion

Flowers behind my closed eyes
A natural love realized
Two child souls dashin'

Echinaceas, magenta
Coneflowers colored polenta
Blazing star firecrackers
Thistles bustle laughter
Coreopsis by hundreds
The prairie, our furry beds

I open my eyes
In your arms I lie
Awake inside
Our love the breezy tide

The Smell of Oxygen

The smell of oxygen fills my lungs
with the scent of electricity charging the feathery grass
down into the spaghetti noodle roots
angels entering in the cracks of Earth as if to wake Her up
for a drink of water from the heavens

A cool breeze awakens the senses of
a dark prehistoric rainforest
the breath of a mushroom
wafting through space and time
to tickle my nose hairs as if to
remind me of a home thousands of miles away

Oxygen's scent is comparable to the whisper of the mourning dove
reminding me that sorrow and melancholy are two colors beautiful
to wear
the fresh cut wood of a once towering and majestic spruce
now stored in a pile for later use

The ether cries, because the sun couldn't rise
through the thick pillows in the sky
a cackle of crows exchange their woes
as this invisible tincture makes us all stronger

As my rain boots glide through
the golden grass of yesteryear
I lend my awoken ear
to the sky
and revel in why
home is where the heart is

The sound of oxygen, that silent wind of a butterfly
the sweet spirits of buttercups
smiling at the falling rain
keeps me wandering far away from here
but I feel so at home

Bee Chase

Have you ever watched a bumble bee chase a honey bee?

The energy is like a great cosmic chase
the beings breaking the rules of time and space

The bumble is the lion of all bees
mighty when mad, but gentle as a breeze

A lone wolf I've come to believe
I see him in solitude amongst the trees

As I water,
he flies thousands of miles per hour
above the droplets on the seedlings
wishing to have a drink

Forwards and backwards, side to side
are just a few ways this guy can glide

The honey bee on the other hand,
is busy as can bee - to help feed his clan

Why's he being chased? He doesn't know,
he just zips around like a UFO

Suddenly they disperse
to flow with the energy of the Universe

Cow Bird Call

The call of the cow bird
Is a unique song to be heard
Melodic and cheerful in nature
Painting quite the otherworldly picture

Variations of chirps and squalls
Melodies alternating, diversity in calls
She tells the stories of another place
Sharing ancient codes of places in space

As we listen, we start to remember
Our souls so deep, a call to surrender
Perhaps she was there, in another lifetime
Sharing her trilly music, surely a sign

She calls to you to bring the codes back
For here and now, our memories in tact
Each joyful and sinuous phrase activated
Our new paradigm, one we create

Late Summer Prairie

As I walk through
        the late summer prairie
        the wary I carry in my heart
        completely vanishes
        as the essence slowly sinks in

My senses come alive
        like a bustling bee hive
        and suddenly I find myself dancing
        spinning in pure bliss

The scent of the late summer prairie
        is dry, pungent, fresh, and fragrant
        like the smell of old leather shoes
        or the herbal aroma of an apothecary

As I pick seeds & scatter them with joy
        I feel my heart open up screaming, more, more!
        They smell so real, so surreal
        the last moments of summer
        and the first scents of fall

Yellows and gold blind my vision
        as the taints of summer diminish
        bees and wasps of all shapes and sizes
        buzz around the blossoms,
        filling me with energy so alive

Fall is Coming

Fall is coming
But I'm longing
For summer to stay awhile longer

I relish in the sounds of the bees
And the rustling breeze between the trees
My heart wants them to last forever

The seasons are changing
Meaning my life needs rearranging
To prepare for the long winter ahead

But no!
Where's the summer everlasting?
Everyday is sunny and warm
And I am left here, with an inner storm

The Secret World of Frogs

September can be exceptionally noisy in nature. Everyone seems to be getting the last of their tasks in before the long season of winter drifts in. Bees buzz frantically from flower to flower, cicadas and crickets chirp their ethereal symphonies, rivers even rush on by.

It was on one of these bustling and sunny days that I found myself immersed in the secret world of frogs.

While everyone else was rushing around, the frogs remained still. Observant. Ever so present with the day, hour, minute, second, though I'm sure frogs have no concept of time. It is an illusion after all.

A trickling creek was omnipresent with these sages, masters of being happy in the present moment. I mean, look at their smiles!

If there is one lesson the frogs have to teach us today, it is that of being present. Of just being. A mission of many people incarnate here today is that of learning beingness and presence. There is nothing to *do*, rather, much to just *be.* It is in our beingness, of being calm and rooted, where we can make the biggest impact on creating New Earth.

Bring this little mantra from the frogs with you today.

"I am rooted in the present moment and all that I am."

Bridge Birch Reflection

A bridge is like a gateway to the land

From behind is a giant body of liquid uncertainty,
a glance
will put you in a trance

For so long,
you've been drifting along,
trying to find your dance

Upon arrival,
your new survival
is the hope imprinted on the mirror

You see the Earth,
She trusts the surf,
with her image cast upon the water

You sigh, "At last!
I can finally rest,"
for the journey upon the water is over

First steps on the ground,
make new sounds,
of roots being planted

Walk over the bridge,
around the ridge,
where the birch trees lay asleep

It's winter now,
nature has bowed,
and sleeps in the cold months ahead

You're awake,
it's no mistake,
magic engulfs your mind

Use your brain,
it's not insane,
to plan for the springtime ahead

Consciousness

Nostalgia Time Travel

On a windy road
The sun glimmers through the trees
While my bike tire hits countless potholes

Crooked oaks reach for the clouds
I always knew they had a deeper part to them
Their acorns and thick leaves create rustling sounds
A travel through time, to way back when

In an instant, it's 1960
And a different world opens up to me
A new, but oh so familiar feeling
Kept my bike tires ever a'reeling

Around a sharp bend I almost crash
And then it opens up to me
A village
Of moss covered roofs

Deserted it was on this day
But yesterday, it was filled with visitors from far away
Little lake cottages
All white with fern green trim
Fuzzy moss covered each roof
Bright as the grass is green
Filling every person with feelings so serene

I transfer my transport to my bare, child feet
And discover the coolness of the stone slab pathways
The stairways
That bring me further into this once upon a scene
The oaks and evergreens shade each cabin
Though through the pockets in the canopy, sun shines ever so brightly

I stand in silence amongst the empty white boxes
Each collapsing in their own way
It is nostalgic, I must say, to stand in a once busy place
And now it's rotting without a human trace
Paint stripping off the walls
Black roofs under mossy carpets dripping into the Earth
Twigs & decomposed leaves create new soil in rusted gutters
Wooded stairs disintegrating under Irish colored paint

The beautiful thing about death, though,
is that it creates new life for new beings
It's bittersweet because my child toes
Know
That this won't be my playground forever
It'll turn into a memory for me to later treasure

A photograph I can bring with me
So I can come back to this moment for all eternity
I turn around to hop back onto my bike
Where I'll continue to flow for the rest of my life

Away from this little whimsical village I go
To discover a new part of soul

Two Friends

Two friends standing on the edge of a cliff
Pondering the mysteries of life, the "what if's?"

What if we go for our dreams?
Will our lives turn out better than it seems?

What if we go big, take those chances?
Will our life be great, each moment enchanted?

What if we work as a team, together?
Let go of competition, embrace collaboration for the better?

What if we're two of the same?
Learning how to be together in this life's game?

You see, there's no competition today
Just chances to help each other, to go out and play

Meeting new souls is like meeting family
Like harmonizing notes in a gentle melody

As we hike this desert terrain

I see you in me, and me in you

We are humanity, one of the same

Awareness

Having awareness of being aware,
Is a sensation of feeling that you're actually here!

A jump start
In the center of your heart

A twinge of magic
Taking your life off automatic

And creating paradise in your present moment

Banjo Adventures

A hopeful tune, on a day so blue
The warm twang of the banjo string
My body feels calm, my mind starts to wander
To places far away, of eternal summer

Is it a trap, perhaps?
Longing for something other than today
Being in the warm sun
Sounds like a day well played

This moment in front of me
Is filled with ice and sleeping trees
My soul knows a happy home
With the bees and summer breeze

With the freedom & ability now
To travel anyway, off the ground
Is it best to stay home;
Or to seek adventure, to go?

Imagining adventure, the trill of the unknown
Pours into the air, through the music just now told
A remembering of what it feels like being free
The pulse of this music, it reminds me

Maybe next winter we'll live adventure
Like we used to, good ol' ramblers
But for today, we choose to stay
And build this better tomorrow
In the meantime and pray

A gaze beyond the trim color pane
Blue, patient and cold
Rose & white for the days of old
A change of perception
Shows other times reflected

Shifting Dimensions

Fallen tree in the path, what to do?
    Turn around, or plow right on through?
Is it a sign from the faeries?
    Are they asking you to be wary?
Or is it just an act of nature,
    The quiet beyond a mystery?

Passing through the forest to become silent.
All winds stop, suddenly the magic surfaces, ambient

What appear to be little insects,
    are actually fairies flying
    going about their ethereal day

They come in all shapes and sizes,
    from little dainty winged creatures,
    to bigger more noticeable features

The dryads serenade in between the calls of the bird,
    with every large tree I see
    knowing they will speak another word.

A twig cracks, "Who goes there?"
    Why it's none other than
    the Green Man,
    not to cause any scare

The invisible creatures of the forest may their intentions be pure,

They only want to make peace with humans, and not cause any fear

Respect and acknowledgement is their wish
    Relationships beyond form, forever to cherish

Stone Lookabout

Any stone you look about
   contains a diverse world, we can't live without
River rocks within them, they contain
   a secret realm hidden beneath the solid vein

A fluorite was found amongst tumbled gems
   in a coconut shell next to a kaleidoscope plant
Calling out to me
   calling to be seen

Upon its surface I cast a breath
   exchanging energy, a hello! It said
And began to glow
   as it awakened so

The sailboat canvas, 'twas shaped
   inside a colorful world, it did take
A scene, a land only on Earth
   a different reality, one must surf

Upon a facet, a crack-et, the horizon
   'twas built a small village frozen in time
On the edge of an ocean
   flowing with the cycles of the tide

In the sky, a band of violet
   cast upon the planet eternal quiet
The teal atmosphere
   make the residents' minds so clear

Turning the stone a little to the left
   is a secret portal, hidden, well kept
Glowing iridescent rainbows
   like an oyster's precious pearls

The residents here create with cerebral calm
   going about their days gently, as nothing's wrong
Evergreen trees casually sip their tea
   and the nature spirits dance mightily with glee

The beings inside, well they do not stride
   for they are made of light, they float to be alive
Just like the facet, each holds that portal in heart
   it is their sacred spirit that creates ethereal art

At night, everyone gathers
   the beings
   the trees
   faeries
   spirits
   even the fishies
The violet band in the sky
   catches a'flame, everyone let's out a cry!
They dance until dawn
   as the embers upon them fall
Adding to their blissful vessels
   renewed life, together a miracle

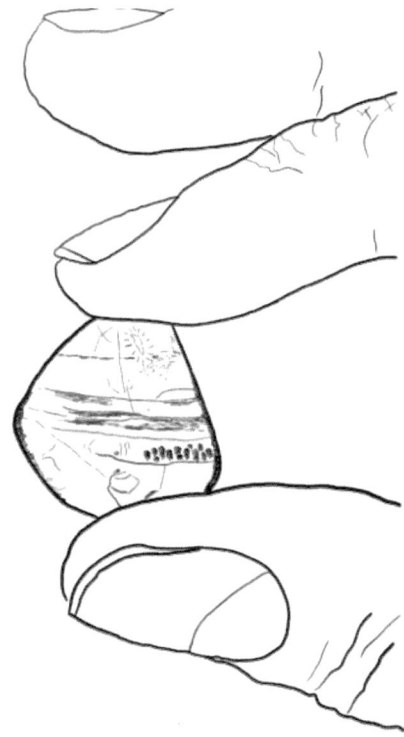

Signs

Whether you believe in angels, the Universe, or spirit guides
Whatever you do - follow their signs!

Subtle things like a honey bee in January
Or a heart shaped rock in a nature sanctuary

Our ethereal friends want to guide us
Down our divine path with unconditional trust

Sometimes they speak to us with symbols and signs
It is, after all, the language of the divine

Listen and follow what they have to say
They are leading you along your soul's way

Ordinary Wonder

Sometimes I feel like I'm not living life
Like I haven't traveled enough, seen enough, done enough
I see others exploring day after day
While I sit at home, pondering if I may

Then I'm reminded
That the glitters aren't gold always
Living in a wonder of the world
Has its time and place

My body feels most comfortable at home
In the simplicity of the mundane
I find the truest parts of my soul
In the everyday plain

Let's go for a walk
And you'll see
Exactly what I mean

In a forest that looks dead as can be
Stick your nose up very closely

Behold! A miniature mushroom!
It's closing for a fairy, a room
Deep inside you will notice
Her picking out her most glorious bodice
Ah, and next to her little tree cavern
Rests a hole in the ground, a secret tavern
Many of the forest creatures visit here
The footprints leading inside make it clear

If your imagination cannot take you far,
Then consider a more realistic perspective
The first flowers of spring can bring you awe
The first tweedle-dees of spring birds, sounds for the rested

We're then reminded that we're enough
By being in the presence of nature
Everything here is imperfectly perfect
She judges no one
Who chooses a simple life
Of going-no-where's
And staying at home in the heart

Naked Showers

It was time for a midday shower
And what better way than under
Nature's expansive power

A feeling of being most alive
Psychoactive, getting naturally high

I strip off my clothes
Excitedly, from my head to my toes

And step out in the torrential downpour
To allow my wild soul to soar

The feeling of the icy rain
Penetrated my skin, transforming any pain

The smell of waterfalls from
An old home far away
Deep in a prehistoric rainforest
Make my body sway

In this, a breath of a damp mushroom
The feathery touch of an ancient fern
The forcefield of a giant spruce tree
Into a new dimension I turn

Together, we transcend space and time
An adventure across doesn't cost a dime

This smell of a damp forest
Brings me back to the shores of Oregon
Where we used to play
All day in the rain

The Pacific Ocean washes over me
As each drop removes the heat
Off my sweaty, vinegary skin

I scrub myself with an ocean sponge
To scrape the barnacles off the day's grunge

To be truly human
Is to forget about the weather being humid
Transcend your consciousness
Into the galaxies and cosmics

As I finish my outdoorsy shower
It's enlightening to feel so empowered
All while rinsing off in the rain
A sensation of being naturally human

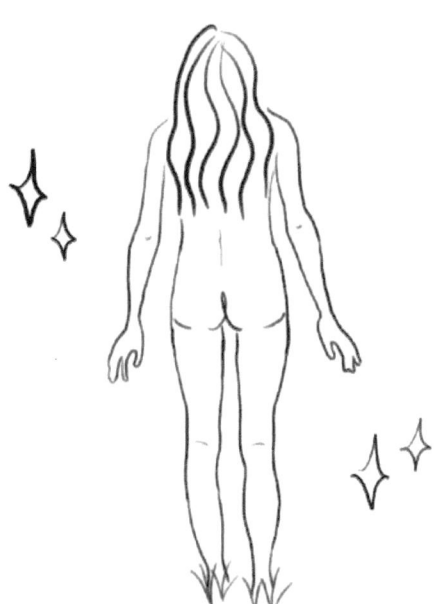

Exploring

On the days where adulting is horribly boring
Jump into your kid shoes and begin exploring!

Bring your journal, some food, a camera in a sack
Run into the forest and don't look back

At some point you'll walk through a portal
That'll transform you into a spirit, no longer mortal

All around you, a new world comes into view
That before a hefty veil had led you askew

Plants moving, growing up towards the clouds
Symphonies created by all the creatures' sounds

A flash goes by! - what you thought were dragonflies
Are actually sylphs, you'll notice, with a double take of the eye

Carpets of feathery ferns, all covered in spherical dew
Sparkles and glitter glisten all around you

Behold! A ring of mushrooms
Another portal to walk through

Where does it go?
Only you will know

Creation Station

Have you noticed how humans are so good at creating things? Think of all the things we create just to make a quick buck. Car washes. Fidget spinners. All things with a "purpose" that also make money.

What if we took that energy to create mindless things and put it into creating things in harmony with Earth? What if we really cared what impact this building or this product had on our planet? What resources are needed to make them? Are you depleting the environment or regenerating it?

Or what if we remembered, our ancestors! Who knew how to solve daily issues without refuse of resources. No uses for fast gratification, since most things took some time and dedication. Many of the problems we face today could be solved by the simplicity of focus, patience, and play. And perhaps reconnecting with their wise and innovative ways.

What do you think the world would be like if most of us thought this way?

The Rise of the Feminine

There's a fire burning. It's all over the world. A fire that is burning down all that is not serving us anymore, humanity, our Earth, and from the ashes a new world is rising.

As the old world burns, I sense a new one rising. It is called the divine feminine. She is fierce. She is free. She is unapologetic of what she feels. All emotions are valid, and are free in this new world. The divine feminine is patient, she knows synchronicity is the language of the Universe, guiding her along her beautiful mission here.

She knows caring for the Earth and humanity comes before profits and economic growth. She knows that she must care and nurture herself before she can do that for others. She feels this deep connection to spirit and her ancestry, knowing deep in her soul who she is and why she came here. She embraces her femininity and allows herself to flow with the cycles of nature. She is creation and creates life. She nurtures Earth like her child, and knows Earth is the mother of all, feeding and nurturing humanity with abundance.

The veil is thin right now. We are so close to the spirits unseen, their messages coming to us so clearly. The other night I dreamt of my dear friend who passed away years ago. In the other world we held hands and exchanged unconditional love. In this moment, I knew that the feminine was coming. And inside of each and every one of us, male or female, is the divine feminine. Who she is lives within each of us right now and it is up to us to allow her to be in our lives.

She calls you when you are tired and need to rest. She gives you that intuitive pull towards the things you desire, with your emotions. She nudges you to make the right choice for the greater good, and to let your demanding ego wash away in the water. Her whispers drift through the wind, calling you outside to connect with Earth with your bare feet, a call of nature that lives within us. We must follow these calls, as our intuition is our guiding light throughout our lives.

The portals are open, choose to walk through and your life will never be the same again. Maybe, just maybe, we will find that deep peace within. That piece you've been looking for. The gentleness and compassion that is always there. This is the chance to build an updated version of Earth, where there is peace all around. Will you join me?

Energies of Earth

The energies coming into Earth right now are super intense and can make our beings feel a range of different things.

Remember to put self love and self care first right now as your body, mind, and spirit adjust. Old energies are coming up to be released, there's no need to be attached to what you're feeling.

Simply acknowledge what is coming up, feel it through, treat yourself with love and respect, and let it all go. Surrender it to the earth, the wind, fire, or water, and allow Earth to take this energy to transmute it.

Give yourself time and space to heal, as this is what you need right now. Flow with the gentleness of your spirit, and the grace in your heart. You are loved. You can do this.

Charging Crystals for Drinks

Find a small crystal for your intention, as simple as quartz crystal, and hold it to your heart while whispering

❋ "May all those who drink this tea,
Be filled with love, light, and serenity" ❋

Drop your charged stone into your drink and allow the vibrational medicine to work its magic. Although the rhyme is for tea, you can use it or adjust it to your needs!

Friends Forever

We had our first snow yesterday
        and I must say
                it was magic that took my breath away

Like twinkles of a high note piano
        crystals fell in a fiasco
                into my soul

Friends forever,
        Sparky and Auggie
                pranced in the field not the least groggy

Cheerfulness burst through the air,
        and suddenly I didn't care

This life we live in, what does it matter?
        We're always surrounded by mindless chatter

But the snow, it knows,
        the real purpose

We're here, to spread cheer
        to be artists, healers, musicians and seers

If IT makes you sad,
        be glad,
                you found the thing to let go of

Cast it free,
        and you will see,
                life beyond the veil

The snow is magic, not tragic,
                embrace your inner calling

Friends forever
        they will treasure,
                this simpler way of life

Ponderings

Do you feel like you're from the stars? You are.

We are all light beings here on a divine mission to help heal each other and the earth.

There is no end to a journey, no end in finding happiness. It is a practice everyday, for today is the only day we have to be happy.

What keeps you from your highest potential and happiness is resistance. Let resistance go and abundance will flow freely to you always.

Ask ✾ Believe ✾ Prepare ✾ Receive

Polarity of LOA

It's very true that our thoughts, feelings, emotions, and beliefs can create our reality. I feel like most people have heard of the law of attraction and have a general understanding of how it works. Basically, our daily thoughts and beliefs shape the reality we live in. We can change anything in our lives with the change of the thoughts & feelings we are having. Things like affirmations, visualizations, meditation and inspired action are great ways to create new realities!

What if though, you have bad days? Will this bring you misfortune?

This is something I've pondered and struggled with for sure. Sometimes I worry that if I have a bad thought, that all the positive work I've done to get to this point will be null. void. Zip! But that's not the reality of it.

The Universe doesn't punish us. We are always experiencing things in divine timing, everything is always working out the way that it's supposed to. Sometimes these thoughts come up so we can process them and claim them to be untrue to our reality, and they can just poof away into the ethers. Sometimes they are hints to look closer at a situation. They are not setbacks. They do not bring us down. Where we are today is always one step ahead of where we were yesterday. We will always receive our desires unless we make the conscious choice to give them up.

Manifestation doesn't have to be strict. In fact, it is meant to be fun and playful! I encourage you to put childlike joy into your day to day, to celebrate and to play along when practicing manifesting something new into your life. The baby steps are worth it. You are worth it. Though the Universe doesn't seem to function with the timing we may want, our manifestations can often come much sooner than we think.

How to Manifest

Ask ❋ Believe ❋ Prepare ❋ Receive

Seed of Life

Have you ever heard of the seed of life? There are many teachings and ancient wisdoms around the seed of life and how it literally creates everything that is in existence today. What I didn't realize, though, that this was something tangible, not just a thought form, that this truly does happen. It was a sort of awakening for me.

Let me explain. The seed of life literally has a consciousness. A consciousness that created the five elements - minerals, water, air, fire/light, and ether. We see and experience these elements everyday. Our bodies are made up of mostly water and minerals, and we need air to fuel our biological operating systems. Most plants and animals on earth are the same way. All of these elements make up all species, including other beings in the universe, each a combination in their own way. Some beings are made up of air and light, their paradigms existing in a different way than ours to where they don't need oxygenated planets to live on, they can live on suns. Other beings are like us in their own way, being different colors and sizes.

Upon learning this, everything changed for me. I felt lighter in a way knowing that life and creation is much simpler than I believed it to be before. Life is funny that way, things are always much simpler than the complexity our minds create reality to be.

Through the seed of life, we are all connected, we are all related through these five elements. Remember this the next time you are faced with adversity, when you feel separate from each other or are faced with beings who may appear scary. We are all one, a part of source, expressing ourselves in unique ways that are all valid and needed.

Mirror Effect

Have you every thought about the mirror effect?

What I mean by that is, have you noticed that what you observe in others, how you may appreciate & admire others is a reflection of an aspect of yourself? Have you ever seen or met someone and thought highly of or liked them for some reason or way?

This concept was revolutionary for me. When I realized this, I became a more conscious observer. I began seeing myself and my good qualities and started appreciating myself more. When I stopped to observe what was going on in my life and noticed how it was tied to my own thoughts and the way I treated myself, I started to shift. I had power to change my life to the way I wanted it to look by changing my self-beliefs & self-talk.

This is a cool tool to use for your lifestyle creation. Notice the good in others, and you will begin to notice the good in yourself. Or vice versa! Appreciate yourself and all of your good qualities! If you meet someone new, know they are a reflection of some aspect of yourself. Send love, gratitude, and kindness and it will come back to you.

Stillness

sometimes
what's best for us
is stillness

being in every moment
observing
the slight curving
of a purple periwinkle

each blink of an eye
feels like a lifetime
as you become aware
of every intricate detail
of the velvety flower petal

in stillness we sponge up consciousness
awareness
of ourselves
and in the ways we've felt lost
we see the path being cleared
and now we're found

Reach for the Colors

Dreams really do come true
they're all inside of you

All you have to do is let them out,
without a doubt

Reach for the colors,
you will find true lovers,
to lift you into the sky

Live for love,
be like a dove
spread compassion and fly

Leave behind
the logical mind

And reach for the sounds of color

A Message of Gratitude

The sun rises rainbows
    painting the sky
A new world before me
    before twinkling eyes
Downstairs I go
    to begin my flow
And thank my body
    for a place to grow
Our souls live inside us
    this body a temple
It loves and it trusts
    our minds will be ample

Life is possible
    with something to live for
That essence around us
    consciousness, a force
It flowers with our feelings,
    our thoughts, the meanings
What we love and adore
    we can expect more and more

Gratitude, gratitude
    a lesson from you
Give thanks for the good things
    and let go of the rest
Gratitude, gratitude
    and uplifting vibration
    the golden force of creation
    of highest manifestation

You Led Me Here

Follow your guides
no matter where they take you
no matter how off path it may seem to you
follow them into
the doorway of your dreams

Lichen Your Life

Lichen your life, it's the only one you got!
Believe in the good things, let go of what's not,
working for you
to become so true

Use the spiritual network,
like a lichen or mushroom perk

We are all connected to the light
that's reflected from the divine source
within us all

Point

Point in the directions of your dreams
and follow the trail
all the way there

Earth Encyclopedia

What if Earth is the encyclopedia, a database of the Universe?

Where each species existing here, has its own planet in another galaxy?

Every insect, ocean creature, reptile, mammal, bird
the dominant specials of their own unique world

And we're all here together, coexisting,
humans already interacting
with extraterrestrials

Could awareness
awaken this truth?

Talking to the Universe

Once you start talking to the Universe
and awaken your soul

Abundance from the inside forms a ball
of snow that begins to roll
slow

There's no going back when
it begins to roll

Your life begins to change
your passions take the reins

All you can do is let go
and let the Universe do its thing

There is inner peace
when you have no clue where you'll go next

Insects Into the Lights

Why is it that insects try so hard to reach the light?
Buzzing against a screen - sending shockwaves of energy through my hair and into my sentience

Wings zapping themselves on screens, the light is in here, in this timeless RV

If they could be in here, would they keep trying, or just be with the light?

We may try hard and seek the source of existence
though we exist with it everyday
it is the sun

The reason we're all alive is because the sun everyday arises

We exist with it, that Lion feeds us
everything we need to trust

To connect with source is to be friends with the sun
spend time outside, have some fun

Let the beetles suffer against weathered screens
as we begin to let go and just be

Abundance Flow

All around me in all directions,
transcending space, time, and past actions

Are beautiful green bills with pyramids on them
a message from the Universe to accept its plan

That feeling of money flying into my life
is like the abundant rain, from a torrential storm during the heat of summer

The nourishing droplets cooling my skin
my natural state of abundance is flowing again

I spin around this money
falling from the sky, giving me plenty

The joy, the unlimited relief
is like the wonder of exploring a coral reef

The green papers smile at me
for now I have an eternal money tree

They bury all my past debts
in the soil below - they are dead

My world is alive and full of life
those green little faeries took away my strife

A chance to live my wildest dreams
this money allows me
to live great deeds
to plant trees
to heal the seas
at any moment I please

Thank you Universe for teaching me this
I now flow in a constant state of bliss

You can have it too
all you have to do
is believe it's true
feel it through

What if...?

What if... the extraterrestrials are already here?
Right under our noses?

People say, my instincts tell me they are around us
But what if they are here, and it is an unveiling of what is in front of us?

The trees who appear dormant and still,
would uproot, show their faces, and walk uphill?

Or the bees,
who defy gravity,
enlarge
to speak to us about the world at large?

I've heard "experts" say that the extraterrestrials are right under our noses

Maybe nature is a mysterious shape shifter

It would be amazing to meet beings from elsewhere
the thought and feeling tickles me like a stream trickles
The UFOs flying in the sky
awaken the soul to ask many why's

Learn to communicate with feelings,
and may you be blessed to have a special meeting

Full Moon Cleanse

On a walk beside the edge of an emerald forest
We set out in a new dimension to explore
In-between - the walls of trees
A stream - trickles evermore

Upon a rickety bridge of stone
The sun through the canopy, it shone

Projecting stars onto the surface of the water
A colorful mirror, showing her lovely daughter

I couldn't resist - I had to go in
To feel the cleansing coolness again

A chance to cool myself of fire
A chance to be reborn in the water

A glide brought me to a patch so wide
Seaweed, so soft on my feet I stride

A feather immersed in emotional water
To sooth her fiery daughter

Adrift over the pebbly floor
I reached the bridge once more

Underneath, a glance from jittery crawfish
Filled my heart with a deeply fulfilled wish

Intergalactic Hug

When you close your eyes as you hug someone,
You are able to experience a miracle

As eyes are closed, you can see
The energy
Of the person you're embracing

The fiery flame of a grounded soul,
Filled with passion for the simple life

Or the iridescent violet glow
of an enchanted forest priestess

The spirits of a million plants coming through
the feet of the energetic healer

A moment in a hug with your eyes closed
you experience the connection more so

A frozen moment in these sacred vibes
lets you know you've found your tribe

Tranquility

Tranquility is my natural state of being

Looking out in the distance is looking within and seeing

The truth cannot be seen on the outside

It's inside, moving like the ocean tides

A Day with the Heart

Everyday when we wake up,
we have a choice to move forward or to stay stuck.

A choice to follow our head or follow our heart,
what you choose determines your start

A day with the head
can take you down a path misled
ego tricks
that build emotional bricks...

A day with the heart,
boy what a start!

Everything falls into place
at nature's pace
and a day of joy abounds.

We all have these abilities,
psychic abilities
that'll awaken if you allow them.

Song of Your Soul

When you're aligned with your soul
Abundance is in continual flow

Life feels easier, effortless, exciting
People may seem more inviting

The birds chirp away with their cheery song
All around you, a symphony to play along

Feeling alive when life is effortless like this
A chance to be immersed in the energy of bliss

Follow the excitement and you will know
The everlasting song of your soul

Inner Divinity

the vibe you dwell in
is the vibe you attract

let out the divinity of you inside
and be surprised
that you meet yourself
right before your eyes

When one door closes, another one opens.

Life is so funny. You can want something, set intentions for something for so many years and then the Universe is like, "Nope, we're gonna do something else!" and closes a door in your life. Something unexpected happens that flips your life around. At all times, we are the stars of our own movies, books, and ironically enough we will never know the full plot!

Go with the flow. When one door closes, there's SO many that open. After crying about the closed door, become aware of the 1,000's of new ones that are opening. You get to choose a new one to go through.

Things of Thoughts

Your thoughts are literally things
Whispering
Creating
Manifesting
Your reality

Allow positive thoughts to flow through
An abundance of life
Will be given to you

Remember

You are
the Universe
expressing itself
as a human for awhile.

Take it easy and have some fun!

Desires & Regrets

Follow your desires
or
live with your regrets

Why so Sirius?

Why so Sirius?
It's easy to connect with us.

We are your star family
You feel us but you can't see

We're from the stars from the perspective of you
We may know a bit more of those universal truths

All you have to do is awaken your mind
Because we are all just beacons of light

We may be extraterrestrial
But we aren't much different than you people

Awaken your mind and it will find
That you're more like us than your kind

We are all a star family
Interconnected in this galactic family tree

Call upon us anytime you wish
Lightning flashes in the distance

Call upon us anytime you please
We'll come over and throw a cosmic party

Intergalactic friends you're allowed to have
Talking to us doesn't make you mad

We're creating this new earth together
So let's have some fun and enjoy the weather

Let this mission unfold for you
Drop all the weight and let your dreams come true

Days of Old

I long for the days of old
Where no one was afraid of the cold
And no one ever did what they were told
I long for those days of old

I long for the simpler days
Where we would sit & watch the willow trees sway
Days, when phones were put away
My heart, it longs for those days

What about times before technology?
When people studied herbology?
And lived with the land, humbly?
Laying in the grass, staring at each other lovingly?

Why do we long for virtual chat rooms?
When people are so lonely all around you?
Why are we afraid of human touch?
When it's a hug that will make us feel enough.

I urge you, this is an emergency
To get back to each other, to show love affectionately
Our bodies are divine don't you see?
Being with each other can never harm you, obviously.

Sovereignty

sovereignty
is key
for evolution of humanity

upgrades come from above
as gentle as a dove
it's up to you to let them in

integrate
don't wait
as you only have here and now

after the download is complete
sit back, make your space neat
and watch the new paradigm unfold

we're on individual journeys
there's no more "saving the planet" worries
as all you need to embody is your divine-self

Mirrors Remember

The world you live in
is a reflection of your inner state
The experiences you have & embody
determine the path you take

We all live in our own paradigms
created by thoughts, feelings, experiences
We shall see in time
A splitting, perhaps, of Earth occurrences

Be honest with yourself
Which path are you on?

Love, bliss, joy, passion, & grace
Never require those feelings amiss

Feelings amiss look like
Fear, hatred, splitting, guilt, shame
Victim emotions
That don't allow the light in

Ask yourself, "Where am I at?"
Being honest with yourself can feel like *splat!*
Or equally as warm as a knit winter hat

We always have the power to choose
The path we walk, the kind of shoes
We walk in,
The paradigm
Of our dreams

Quartz Crystals

the answers you seek are always within you,
connect with your inner light to reveal your truth

lovely lemurian quartz crystals
contain the memories of civilizations
from long ago
that you were a part of

remember, remember, remember

the ancient codes
ways of being
from those lifetimes
bring the truths here and now
and create heaven on earth
by being that which is truth to you

Something Grounding

It dawned upon me
During a rainy afternoon
While listening to 70's music
And editing videos

A mantis peers in behind me
To let me know
That what grounds people to their planet
Is culture
Any type of culture

Being rooted in a culture
Something that is relatable
Something that is group-worthy
Something that brings belonging
Is what is most grounding to a soul

For me
It is listening to 70's music during the summertime
Dancing in the kitchen
Being a tinker-bot, fixing shit
Hanging out in garages in the afternoon heat
Riding in old vehicles because we love the thrill they bring

Being a free spirit, screaming old music
on country highways
passing no one along the way

Dressing in old, unusual clothes
Because they feel authentic and true me

Feeling free in my heart
Belonging to a place
"Under cover" so to say
The culture seemingly predictable
Because it is so familiar to the soul

Treasure Chest

I'm one with the moon
Shimmering shadows dancing in the room
For her, silver is just enough
You don't have to be so tough

What are the answers
To the lizards roaming the night sky
The stars have flown to this place
You and I, two of the same face
Words can't tell you why

Open the buried treasure chest
Let's see what we've cast to rest
What we let the mold get to the old
Is a garden brighter than gold

Do you dare to look inside?
Don't be afraid, you cannot hide
Once you feel the Universe inside
It's clear, all shadows are made of light

Skin & Bones

We are made of skin and bones
but our souls are not bound by this
Only the stars know,
What true love really is

Gardening Scene

Amongst tomato plants so gold & green
I'm able to see a world unseen
New colors, shapes, energies & beings
That woke those extraterrestrial feelings
I think of our friends from outer space
Each with unique colors, complexions, and face

As I weed the ground of life unwanted
A new and scary friend my eye spotted
Longer than my finger
With a horn on his keister
A big juicy horn worm
Between my fingers he did squirm

Upon the leaves, little pellets of poop
From various caterpillars above, they did droop
At first, I added them to my soap bucket
To kill them off for causing a ruckus

I wondered what they turned into
Their colors were orange and crimson blue
Above my eye, a silent cry
From a kaleidoscope butterfly

Up close, she understood, she let me come
And tiptoed on my hand with a purring hum
Her colors were like those of a rainbow child
Black, orange, & blue, colors so wild
I admired her beauty, trust, and grace
And then it clicked for me - they were the same
As I let her go, a decision I made
Not another caterpillar I'd kill, I am sane

I shrieked & cried
Oh what a scary guy!
He rested on the ground in peaceful reply

His existence here, was so simple and clear
He'd eat and transform into a butterfly

Feelings of disgust and uncomfort
Of such an ugly creature of sorts
Made me throw him in the pail
Where his end a green puke he did wail

Immediately I felt guilty
For we share this Earth, he is one with me
Who am I to decide if he lives or dies?
That is the divine's job, not mine

I kept on going with my work anyway
"For the good of all," I did say
"Duties of the farm," something for the day

Despite inner conflict about life and death
I had to let go, continue on my path

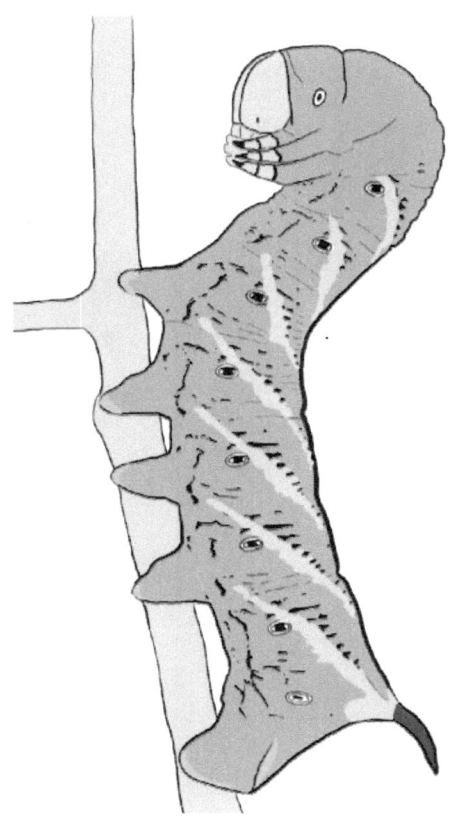

A Message of Gratitude

The sun rises rainbows, painting the sky
A new world before me, behind twinkling eyes

Downstairs I go, to begin my flow
And thank my body, for a place to grow

Our souls live inside us, this body a temple
It loves us, it trusts, our minds will be ample

Life is possible, with something to live for
That essence around us, consciousness, a force

It flows with our feelings, our thoughts, the meanings

What we love and adore
We can expect more and more

Gratitude, gratitude
A lesson from you
Give thanks for the good things
And let go of the rest

Gratitude, gratitude
An uplifting vibration
The golden force of creation
Of highest manifestation

Self

Self Love is Currency

Self care is a path to unlimited abundance

Love yourself and the Universe's love will mirror back to you

To love another, we must love ourselves. To care for another, we must care for ourselves. To feel happiness for another, we must feel happiness within ourselves. It is within ourselves that we find the peace we seek in the outer world.

Doubts

In life, we all have some doubts
We have these visions, dreams we can't live without!

Can we help each other with our talents and gifts?
Are we enough to show we're legit?

Self doubt is one thing, that voice inside your head
Something that can bug you until your dreams are dead

But what if someone else doubts you?
Boy, that's a feeling that'll make you blue

Though instead of feeling blue, why not feel orange and red?
Your heart a burning fire to inspire a dream once dead

Doubt from others isn't a put down for you
It's a sign that they're too feeling blue

Use it to act, dream, perform twice as hard
Achieve the dreams and give them the inspiring card

We are meant to pursue the unique dreams inside us all
It's up to us to follow them, work through the doubts & make that call

You can do it, believe in yourself
And inspire yourself with the doubts

The Essence of Us

Late mornings
Staying in bed
Sleeping in
You get up first instead

I lay awake
With my eyes closed
Wondering what we're doing today
After I put on my clothes

You're somewhere out there
Doing your own thing with the morning
While I lay in bed some more
Hopefully not snoring

The birds share their music
As we make some sort of breakfast
Then the sound of a blue's lick...

I forget the rest.

Mirage Tune – A Song

All these leaves flowing by me on this busy steam,
what can I do but dream

Those crimson colors beaming,
on this busy stream

Mhmm, mhmm

Fish jumping out of water,
the river's daughters

The simple life is great,
you don't have to walk on a path so straight

Why are we here
what do we do
it's up to you to decide
It's all inside

In the forest with my dog,
adding more places to my travel log

I've been all over the globe,
oh oh oh oh

All the places you'll go if only you'd tell yourself so

The path is great,
can you relate?

Just do
what your heart says it true

Memories Song

Memories
Can I just live you once more please
I promise I'll cherish these
In the moment with reverie

Sometimes moments just go on by
We don't know they're important until they're gone in the sky
Sometimes I can only ask myself, "Why, why, why
did I let this go by?"

We can capture a memory, right in the moment
With a pen and a paper, and a shady spot chosen
Sometimes a photo or two will do
I'll add it to our collection, with a little glue

Memories
Can I just live you once more please
I promise I'll cherish these
In the moment with reverie

Some memories just stick to our brain
And we'd rather stop, living them again
The regrets, the losses, the conflict and pain
Can make a person insane

Memories
Can I just let go of you please
I promise I learned my lesson this time
Can I let go of this load and move on with my life?

Run Away, or Stay?

I sit here in these woods thinking about what could be, would be
Feeling like I'll never get there just sitting here now
Running away is what I'm used to
Traveling to the ocean blue
Across wild deserts and forests with you

The answer isn't running away,
it's learning how to stay

Build my roots up here,
is the path that's the most clear

Clarity's trail is the hardest one to achieve
But I know that I can do it, I just gotta believe

Live large

Live large.
Live on the edge.
Travel today because you might not live till tomorrow.
Decide to dream the biggest and best things for yourself.

Then go do it.

Surprise yourself by the bold things you come up with.
Laugh at how crazy it'll feel to do something so liberating.

Go streaking.
Go skinny dipping.

Sleep under the stars in the middle of the desert.
Kiss someone under a waterfall.
Climb the side of a steep cliff to see a remote oasis.
Climb the tallest tree you can find.
Drive 100 mph through curvy sand roads in the desert.

Do wild and crazy things now, because when you're old you'll appreciate the fulfilling life you've lived.

Chase your dreams now because life is short, and flies by in the blink of an eye.

Take chances because there's great rewards.
Be a rebel against your fears and you'll find yourself flying through the stars

Take action because talking about it isn't fulfilling.
Live the life you dream.

Inner Song

I just keep on moving along
Walking to the beat of my own inner song

May twelfth, Two Thousand Nineteen

I really enjoy days like today. Sparky on my lap at the tranquil Oak Creek - upon the red stone I was on two weeks ago. Our adventure started downstream where we hopped along the rocks poking out of the river. I was nervous to go across this one part that was a bit slanted and far from me, so I handed Austin the camera and my phone and made it across with a leap! Sparky became brave and actually walked through the rushing water most of the way down - knowing how icy cold it was. At one point, we settled and he sniffed through the water. Austin almost had him rolling for a treat on a pyramid rock in the center of the creek. The whole canyon is so green with all sorts of textures and shades - the deep crimson jagged bark of the ponderosas. It's days like today that I live for. My highest excitement. The days I can just BE.

Flow and Flux

Life is a constant flux of changing perspectives.
Redefining yourself is a journey that lasts an eternity.

Seeds

A dream is a dream
No matter how small
A dream is a seed
Ready to bloom and grow tall

Wonder

May there be wonder
Wherever you go
Hike the world around you
No matter how slow

You see beauty in the trees, rivers, lakes and streams
Beauty to share from your heart
For all eternity

Personal Vow

Make a vow
to yourself now,
only do things that serve your highest good
your mission here on Earth

Do this
and
your life will be full of worth

You're the Sun

Be resilient
when the going gets rough

You'll be the sun
that shines out of the storm

Forgiveness of the Moment

The crickets tell me to give you a second chance
Things aren't what they seem at first glance
Holding onto anger and resentment
Sometimes feels easier than love and forgiveness

The hawk flies
High in the sky
Catching a warm winter breeze
Reminding me why... We're on this journey together
Sorta like buddies on a winged bird's feather

The mushroom on the tree
Says to be still, let it be
Though time isn't "real"
It's the passing of it that heals

Though now we may be floundering in a flooded desert wash

Hold my hand,
Eventually in the sand
We will land

Physicality

One day I desired to leave the matrix
      surely, for my life? This was the perfect fix
The matrix was a trap, I clearly did see
      shackles that held me in 3D mentality

So onward I went! Head full of dreams
      I quickly learned the powers inside of me
The ability of my thoughts creating reality
      was all I needed to know to set myself free

So I quit my jobs, I quit working!
      and traveled around with minimal needs
A lot of baggage, I did carry inside
      all too heavy to allow me to fly

Along my journey I lightened my load
      faced my fears! For me, so bold
Learned much about the conscious universe
      that within me, lost memories did stir

Within me awakened a higher perspective
      cosmic beings, within me, were reflected
Realizing we're all so infinite, souls without boundaries
      many lives we've lived, each of us a living library

Somewhere along my journey, I left the Earth!
      forgot what it meant to be here, have worth
Sometimes a higher vibration is all it takes
      to have purpose here, to make a change

A new desire I felt inside
      to become physical, once again, & sway with the tides
The 3D matrix felt like hopeless fate to me
      but creating beauty in the physical is my destiny

Faulty Failures

The things we do in life can sometimes feel like failures. All our hard work, passion, put into something and it just fails. Or that's our perspective of it anyway.

Anything you do straight from your heart is NOT a failure, it is a win. Anything from your heart is an act of love for yourself and the people around you that fills you up with joy. Maybe you don't get those ego things (money, power, sex, fame...) every time you follow your heart, but you definitely make yourself richer and more alive when you do. Our society portrays that to be successful in life, you need those four ego outcomes to show it, but I digress. If you want to do something from your heart, just do it. Maybe those things will or won't follow, but I'm telling you that success is a rich and warm heart.

A "failure" today can turn into a success tomorrow. That thing you do that makes your heart sing can be a baby step to something greater, even if you can't see past the horizon.

What is Happiness?

Is it being around others who make you happy?
Is it having a close knit family?

Is it a certain place on earth?
Is it a job that makes you fulfilled and full of worth?

Is it the constant move, nomadic travel?
Or miraculously allowing your life to unravel?

Is it a hobby, a heart's calling?
Or is it that lovely person who's kept you falling?

Is it having a spirit so wild and free?
Or being content sitting under a grand oak tree?

Is it doing nothing at all, being in solitude in a forest so tall?
Or is it being in a bustling city, where at night the lights are pretty?

Is it writing a song, that many others sing along?
Or serving the community, spreading a sense of unity?

Is it standing for a cause, living for it day by day without a pause?
Or being a kind neighbor, someone to depend upon spreading kindness and cheer?

Whatever it is that makes you happy,
Do it with all your heart.

Live in it with everyday presence
Because there is no tomorrow or yesterday.

Just today.

If you're not happy,
Consider this
It's never too late to follow your dreams
To do anything with happiness as the means

There is only today
The perfect day
To have a smile on your face

Love is

Love is writing poetry as you play the music of your soul,
& laughing hysterically as our naked bodies dodge the raindrops of a summer storm

Love is smelling your musky hair as your head lay on my beating heart

And climbing a tall mountain just to see the sun through the pass

Love is believing in you, even when a lot of days you're in those grey sweatpants eating brownies
& laughing at what's going wrong because there's nothing else we can do

Love is a screaming dog in the backseat excited to go hiking
And the way you hold my hand when we're out walking

Love is intending to go on a long nature journey
And instead hopping river rocks in the sun in our undies

Love is looking into your blue eyes
And realizing we've chosen unique lives

Love is knowing the journey is unknown and confusing
And finding the light to make it amazing

Love isn't a destination you see
It's in the present moment who you choose to be

A Midnight Pondering

It is humbling to know that the quiet people can have a special place in the world. A place where they can share their quietness and others can join in, to appreciate slow and silent moments. At times I can be loud and expressive of that, but others I just keep my mouth closed and express myself in other ways, quieter ways. And I'm humbled I can be both, both are acceptable by me, and I can be both those versions of me when they come. It's so very humbling.

Open Eyes, Open Heart

rest often,
laugh much,
life is much better,
with our hearts in touch.

we don't know the answers for tomorrow
and that's okay.
what matters most to me,
is how we spend each day.

life is worth living
each moment our eyes are open
each felt emotion
with the present words that are spoken

the greatest treasure on Earth
is an open heart who knows its worth

go for it big, with all your might
you are an empowered human being
look inside yourself, it's something worth seeing

Celebration Contemplation

Often times in life we decide to go go go. Many times we burn out, crash, or feel like we're never enough. It's great to strive and accomplish but what about the ability to celebrate? What about the ability to stop and to let all of your successes and accomplishments catch up with you?

Today I was reminded of this. That I have come so far yet all that I have accomplished hasn't caught up to me yet. So I decided to stop. To look around me. After a strong thunderstorm, I took my dog with me into the woods to walk through the puddles of water on the trails. To stop along the way and to whistle with the birds, and for them to whistle back at me. It reminded me that all that I put out in the world comes right back.

Knowing and experiencing this now I realize, that what I do is like a ripple. All that I have done is still getting out into the world. And maybe I can't have instant gratification. Maybe all the work that I have done has led me to this moment right now so I could experience the feeling of celebration and the feeling of living in the moment and living within the pulses of the trees and the insects all around me.

Yeah sometimes life gets rough. All that you have worked on could seem like it's falling right through the floor. But all is not lost. Nothing is ever lost. No, it is just waiting to be discovered. All you have ever wanted to be and all that you are is here in this moment. You just have to look within and see

Grand Oak Tree

You are to me
A grand oak tree
Humble and strong as can be
Branches secure and out so wide
In a field of serenity

Your bark was crinkled,
From worries, those wrinkles
You no longer need to endure
We're so happy for you
To let go, to know the truth
To be free forever more

In any storm, wind tustling through
Your leaves, your everyday life
Didn't shake the roots you grew
In the Earth below you

In the most beautiful of summer days
You were calm, protecting your sapling understory
Making sure that all their lives they'd be protected, to leave a legacy

But that's just the thing, dad
You left such a legacy in the way you were to others
Always looking out for them,
caring for them like the most noble of fathers

You spent your days loving your kin,
your little saplings below your branches
Teaching us what you know
Teaching us how to grow

And now that you're gone, your branches bare of leaves
Your legacy of what you started remains right under you,
to grow a whole new forest of oaks,
To continue what you started

Our roots intertwined with yours
Saplings rooted, holding on tight
To the morals, the lessons, the experiences
You left in the soil

Though in the physical, you're here no more
Your spirit is in the air, like a bird to soar
The thing with spirit is it never grows old
It is eternal, I was once told

You are always here for us,
Always in our hearts
Your spirit flowing through the wind
and creating sparks

Thank you for all you did in your life
For living fully,
Creating your family,
Following your dreams,
For being sincere
We will always remember you
Because in our hearts, you're still here

A poem for my dad
8/5/1963 - 4/5/2019

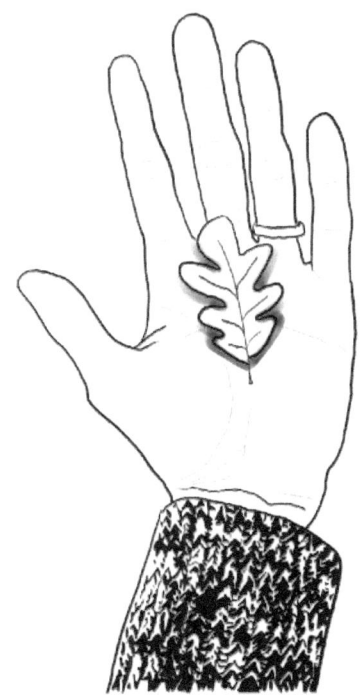

Mirrors

People are mirrors
They show our biggest strengths
And our inner fears

Comparing and Sharing

There's no use in comparing
Our reasons here are for sharing
The uniqueness each of us holds
Needs to be let out and told

Sundays

Do you remember the feeling of Sundays as a kid?
Waking up on a warm spring morning, winter not quite finished
But the air, so warm, that ye must go out and explore

That feeling of school starting tomorrow,
but there's so much outdoors
today

Hopping onto a bicycle,
riding down to the lake on windy roads
budding trees
a melting pond breeze
short sleeves
getting lost in time

What to do?
Could throw a line in off the bridge
See what kinda fish are biting today

Or play tennis with archaic wooden racquets
vines growing all over the fence and nets
At a crackling, abandoned court
Conquered now as a child's fort

Like visiting Alice in her land down the rabbit hole
What about getting lost in the woods?
And climbing pine trees
to have the best view anyone could see?

A whistle in the distance, it's time to go home
Spend the night doing homework in a blanket dome
Holding onto as much as this day as possible
The dread of school the next day could swallow...

The sun sets, a rainbow of hues blanket the sky down to a solar hideout

Sunday
A good day
To just be a human and play

Free Spirit

I have this insatiable desire to go streaking out in the middle of nowhere, where no rules exist. Where no authorities roam. To feel completely free, limitless, the ultimate joy. And my wish is to share this experience with like minded friends who would galavant along side me, grins beaming on their faces and just running in the freedom that we are. The ultimate act of just "being."

When the Going Gets Rough

Sometimes when I feel low, I retreat, and find myself creating and sharing less and less. It is always my intention to uplift and inspire people with my words, and when I feel defeated or doubtful I don't feel of service to anyone.

But let's get real here, nobody is perfect. I am not perfect and I'm totally okay with having flaws and having difficulties. And it is okay and safe to share these times because it helps others feel that they aren't alone in their hard times.

I suppose my words of inspiration for you today are:

❋ **When the going gets rough, if things don't seem to be working out, take a break but don't give up!** ❋

Sometimes, we can feel on a roll, getting past challenges and having victories... only to be slapped in the face with another challenge. It can feel like a never ending cycle of this, and we may wonder if it's even worth it at all.

I want to tell you it IS worth it! It's okay to feel angry. Scream at the top of your lungs about how pissed you are! Acknowledge your feelings and promise yourself never again. These times seem to be filled with lessons, with happenings that make you question yourself and your motives. This can help with inner work, with learning more about yourself and how you want to move forward, what matters most in your life?

Something I'm practicing more often is self-love in the form of pampering myself. Rose scented baths. Immersive journaling. Simple crafts like crocheting. Nourishing foods. There are so many ways to practice self-love, I encourage you to join along!

Know that this too shall pass, hang in there friends. We can make it!

Truth Chant

Anything rooted in fear is furthest from the truth my dear

Beginning the Truth

When you're in this beginning stage of following your inner truth, it can feel like you're in a dungeon, and quite literally, you could live in a space that feels that way, reflecting your inner feelings. You may identify this way because you aren't super knowledgeable about that which you want to pursue, or have internal rooms of your multidimensional body-house filled and cluttered with old, useless things. Living your dreams can be confusing sometimes, a matter of trying new things to find out what works for you and what doesn't.

There is going to be a time when you get into a really light space. It is a practice - learning what you need and how you would like to proceed, and letting go of that which does not serve you. How are you going to practice being the light in the dark; how are you going to be the candle light in the dark room? How can you light yourself up, from inside, to illuminate your own way? What is in your body-house that doesn't need to be there; what can you see now that you can release and give back to Spirit?

Eventually, the shades open up in that dark room and then you realize you're not the only light in the room anymore; you have light coming in. Others find you and are attracted to your bravery and illumination and find you as a guide along their paths in their dark rooms. After cleaning out your body-house you will have room for new things, new people. Be the light for others. Be the light for yourself. You will find that it is always worth following, and that it'll always take you on your highest path.

Resilience

Resilience is key
for everyone to succeed

Through thick and thin,
with resilience you'll always win

Be true to yourself
and you'll attract an abundance of wealth

Resilience is a way
to keep going throughout the day

A chance to keep trying
even though inside you may be crying

Resilience is focusing on your goal
even though it's hard on your soul

Because deep down,
if we don't pursue our heart's desires,
we will drown

So choose resilience
and give your dreams a second chance

Are You Ready?

I'm ready, are you ready?
    Our lives are everything but steady

Change is inevitable, almost every day
    how you respond is a choice you make

Embrace change with a ready stance,
    bold and open to take a chance

Rewards will follow
    either in joy or sorrow
    both beneficial to our being

Cringe and hide,
    inside you may cry
    Resistance to change will make you ask why?

Go with the flow,
    surrender to the Universe and let go,
    and your life will be a balanced river shown

The Heart of Winter

In the heart of winter
you'll find your peace

Realize, reflect, and embrace
what you feel

Remember your mistakes
and let go

Drift into the magic
within your soul

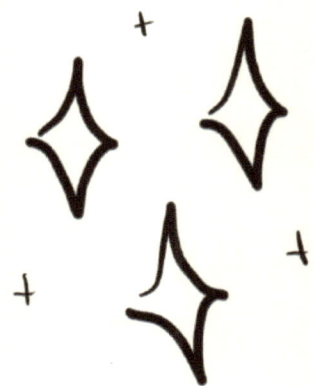

Uncertainty and Faith

Uncertainty can free you,
but faith will ease you

Surrender

Surrender to the Universe
 and accept all the gifts
  She brings

Be Deciduous

In a forest of pines
 be a deciduous
  that changes
   with the cycles of nature

Warrior

Be a warrior
get stuff done
feel empowered
you got this

In life we have chapters. Cycles. There's a beginning and an end.

Getting to the end of a chapter may have you feeling like you want to skip over it. It feels like too much work. Overwhelming.

I'm here with you. Feeling this. Knowing what's on the horizon and wanting to just get there.

But here's the thing... if you read a book with missing ends to the chapters, it wouldn't make much sense, would it?

Finish the chapter strong. Be your best. Be that warrior. Be your own hero. Living's in the journey not the destination.

Feel Into Yourself

When your body is tired from doing your passion
you are growing stronger, showing your dedication

When your mind is tired and you want to sleep
You spent your day well, you need rest

When the Universe gives you something other than a want
it is giving you just what you need

Personal Truth

It is your own personal truth that sets you free
what your soul craves on the inside
releases the external shackles of misery

Imagine your best life
in your mind's eye

Reality is what you create it to be
just accept, don't ask why

Everyone's dreams are different, you see
so let go,
imagine,
feel who you are truly meant to be

Your Time

When all you want to do is hide
remember, it is YOUR time

You are worthy of being seen
the other side of this fear,
my dear,
are feelings of love and serene

You, and what you have to say is important
let it out, be loud, be authentic

Those scary feelings inside aren't yours
let them flow out of you and into the floor

Be Like a River

Be like a river, and go with the flow
Life becomes jollier when we allow and let go

Become deep like the river and explore yourself
Healing your pain gives your life much wealth

Bend like the river and flow where it feels best
Follow the love that serenades your heart in your chest

Grow like the river when the rain pours down
Accept the abundance, your life becomes sound

Please yourself like the mighty stream
Open your mind's eye to the greatness now to be seen

Be like the water and reflect the stars at night
Show your fellow humans we are all made of light

Silent Healing

So often, things are healed without a word spoken
In a moment
All answers are revealed and a resolution happens by feeling it
And in a flash
The wound is healed and awakened

You're Enough

Feeling that you're enough
Can sometimes be tough
With the expectations set upon us

But let me tell you, a universal truth

All of you is enough

You can sleep, dream, cook and read
that's enough to fill a day
Relaxing and caring for yourself
Keeps stress at bay

The body you were given, could not be chosen
And that's totally okay
You are you, she is she, he is he,
Nobody is the same

Celebrate your uniqueness and know
That you're the only one in the Universe

No one can be you
that's your job to do

You are special, you have an important mission
You were put here to do
Unfold your life, let go of strife
And discover that authentic truth

Content

It's been so long since I've felt this happy and in love with life, consistently, and for it to be my balanced state.

❀ Everything is happening best case scenario ❀

❀ All is in divine order ❀

❀ Life feels like grace, love, fun, and play ❀

are just some of the things I remind myself everyday. It took a lot to get here, to figure out what "happiness" means to me, and to just do it. To just go for my dreams. It's not all figured out, I still find the challenges, but you know what? Who cares. It's definitely a blast and totally empowering.

May this reflection of me integrate into you.

Shadow Self

our shadow side is not our flaws, no
our shadow side are the parts of us that wish to be discovered

in the void, there are endless possibilities
quantum possibilities
embracing both polarities

this is where our shadow lives

we can venture inside to discover
that part of us with divine, true power

tiptoe along the twilight forest path
meet many aspects of you along the track

glowing in the darkness
is your essence

that shadow self of yours
is actually a radiant light, forevermore

will you step on that path to find you?

Shadow

A part of me I never show
A part of me that seems quite unconventional
A longing wish looking deep into the sky
A dream that doesn't need to answer why

Rest

rest
you must
to enable self trust

the polarities of being human
of being and doing
come to balance
when we stop
and rest

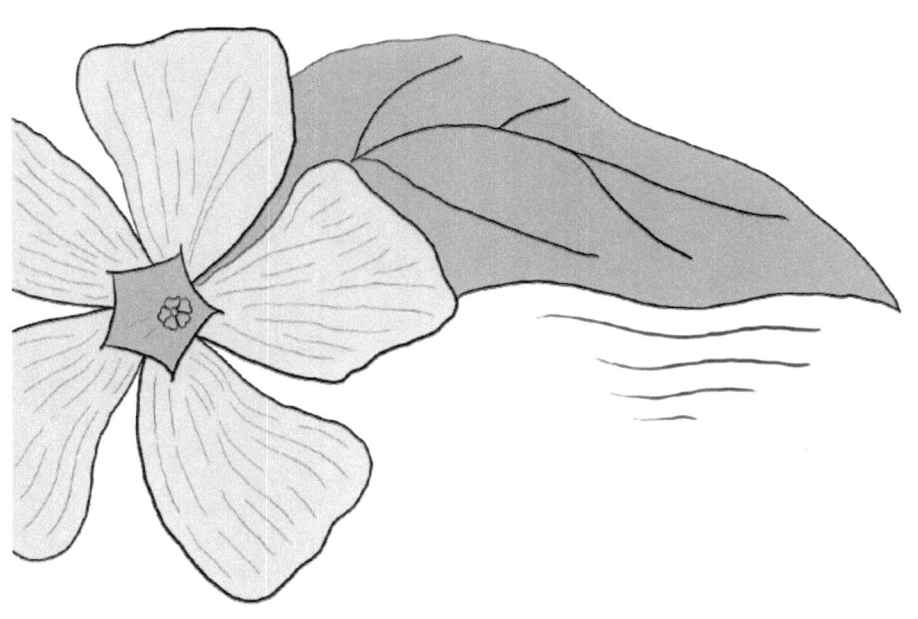

Strange Me

allow yourself to be who you came here to be
even if you think it looks strange to those around you, that see

the secret is, don't do it for them my dear
do it for you, to be a being so clear

when they ask about you, don't fret
the understanding will be met

explain yourself with grace & love
and your inner self will fly like a dove

Sweet Surrender

Here's to the ones who never grow up
Who dream big & who never stay stuck
Age is a number, don't let it define you
We choose to get older, that's a divine truth

The dreamer is the one who never ages
She just advances to higher stages
She dreams big, and it manifests
All while feeling like her personal best

The journey to the dream is usually tough
It's a test of time to feel confident enough
Do you, to your standards, have what it takes to live in that state?
When you decide that you do, your life becomes great

The road to get there is a mindset shift
A mental house that you build with positive bricks
Fill yourself up with feelings of love
To soar above the old you like a dove

When you're on this path there's one thing left to do
Surrender to the Universe, let it all flow to you
Let your fears go, go with the flow
Take those chances that'll make you grow

When you've done the best you can
Sit back and let the Universe unfold its plan
It's the most important part to remember
Believe in yourself and surrender

Moving On

When something's magic starts to fade
It's okay to say "thank you," and walk away

The experience that manifest has finished, it was had
Store away the good times,
There's no need to whimper and feel sad

Be grateful for the people you met
They'll be the ones you'll never forget

Gripping on can hold you behind
Keeping you in a box, lifeless, confined

Ask for ease and grace
Listen to the Universe's signs
Imagine new dreams, a new place
A new cycle begins, in this time

Emotions

When our emotions are feeling especially low
it's okay to stop and take it slow

Often times
We may not know why
These abyssal emotions arise

The best thing to do
Is rest, allow healing around you
And to feel all of this through

Know that it will pass
Sometimes slow, sometimes fast

Allow yourself to feel this way
Whether it's for an hour or a day
It is not here to permanently stay

Give yourself the gift of movement
Dancing in the moment,
Breaking off chunks of the past
That have become stagnant

All emotions were created equally
Energy, naturally, flows neutrally
All from the Universe for expanding & healing

Give yourself a hug
Fill yourself with love
And know you're a Divine Being

A Lasting Reminder

Remember to be gentle with yourself

Remember how far you've come

Remember you're a divine spirit living in a human body

Remember that you too have feelings and to be kind to yourself

Remember that anything worth pursuing takes time, persistence, patience, and lots of love

Remember to pursue grace and inner peace over hype and "hustle bustle"

Remember to take your time and to take it slow, time isn't real anyway

Things may feel heavy in the world right now. Our traumas and triggers are coming up not to trigger us, but to remind us of how far we've come, & to let them go to make room for the new. Spring clean out your innards and allow new blooms to rise up out of the dark womb of soil we've been percolating in all winter long. Our time is here, growing pains are totally a thing, and here we will rise like the phoenixes we are.

That's all folks!

Thanks so much for reading Find Me in the Forest.

My wish for you is to live your lives in harmony, peace, and bliss, and to become aware to the dimensions, worlds, and beings all around you at all times.

Much love and light on your journey!

❋ Ash ❋

Other Books by Ashley Lynn

A Year Against the Rain

Morning Motivations

The Adventures Across Guided Journal

The Adventures Across Zine-A Series of Cosmic Guides

Visit Adventures Across Online!

Visit the online shop for whimsical art prints of nature & metaphysics and my other books; the blog for inspiring & spiritual stories of simple living as an awakened soul here on earth; and find informative & artistic videos about a range of topics from foraging & permaculture -to- metaphysics, magic, and spirituality.

www.adventuresacross.com

 **Ashley Lynn** Is a writer, poet, photographer, plant enthusiast, artist, and mystic exploring Earth out of Wisconsin. She has self published several books, created hundreds of videos & films, written music, started food forests, awakened ancient knowledge, and traveled all over the planet as a spiritual nomad. Ashley cares deeply about living paradise, taking care of Earth, and sharing her art with the world.

↓ ↓ ↓ Read about my story and mission here on Earth ↓ ↓ ↓
www.adventuresacross.com

Art/Photography prints, Zines, sessions & more at
www.adventuresacross.com/shop

Feel free to tag @adventuesacross and leave feedback on my website or Amazon to share your experiences and stories with any of my books! Leaving a review means others can find this book too!

www.adventuresacross.com/contact

Amazon Author Page

www.ingramcontent.com/pod-product-compliance
Lightning Source LLC
Chambersburg PA
CBHW020534080526
44583CB00013B/859